THE HEART OF A LEADER

SIMENE' WALDEN

Published by Simene' Walden

P.O. BOX 813, SAVAGE, MD 20763

© 2021 Simene' Walden

ISBN: 978-1-7357977-9-3

To book any other authors, please contact them directly.

If you are interested in discounts for bulk purchases or to use any part of this book, please email:
simene@simenewalden.com

Cover Design by Mizigns

Editing by J. Flowers Olnowich

First Printing October 2021

Printed in the United States of America

The Heart of a Leader Contents

DEDICATION

To our youngest leader, Hairston Elijah Hamilton born while this book was being birthed. Your mommy has set a great legacy before you.

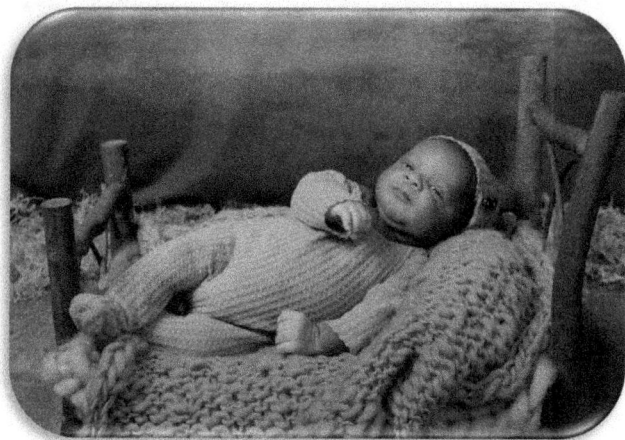

Our Miracle Baby was very fortunate to be here. The umbilical cord was wrapped around his neck twice and tied in a knot. The doctor said this was very alarming and could have been fatal, but God has bigger plans for him. We have a special little man with a purpose and a plan. Born 8/18/21 @ 8:18 am weighing 8 lbs.

— Mommy & Daddy

ACKNOWLEDGEMENTS

The most important thank you goes to my God, Yahweh, for the gift of life and another day to fulfill purpose and not waste my years on this earth. Thank you Abba! Thank you to each co-author for your expertise and leadership abilities that you saw fit to share in this project. Each of you are peculiar in your own way and wonderfully made. May great doors of exposure and opportunity come your way for the seed you have sown with your writing in this anthology. Thank you Dr. Levatta for being our foreword author and blessing this book with your words. Your "Yes" meant more to me than you will ever know. More grace and blessings to you as you continue to make a leadership impact in this world and in the academic space. Thank you to each person who has ever given me the opportunity to lead. Thank you for trusting me to lead and to lead well. Each time I was charged with the responsibility to do so, it stretched and grew me. Thank you to each of you who have purchased this book, who will read it, and apply it to your life accordingly. May leadership elevation be your portion now in Jesus' Name.

Visionary Author

Simene' Walden

FOREWORD BY

Dr. Levatta L. Dean Levels

Let me first say *The Heart of a Leader* is anthology of beautiful, transparent, and relevant narratives written by outstanding leaders in many careers. The stories are incredibly poignant, stimulating, heartwarming, personable, and relatable.

After reading *The Heart of a Leader*, I'm reminded of Nehemiah discussed in *The Holy Bible*. Nehemiah's life provides a superlative study on leadership. Nehemiah displayed the wisdom of an effective leader. He used his administrative skills in his strategies as an effective leader to guide the reconstruction of a city in the most hostile of climates. In addition, he had leadership traits, characteristics, and values that established him as one of the most outstanding leaders of the Holy Bible. Nehemiah exhibited a steadfast determination to complete his goals which resulted in people being encouraged, renewed, and excited about their future. His story was a reflection of his heart as a leader.

The Heart of a Leader is a guide and a calling. The focus is a navigation that maps the journeys through leadership successes, failures, mountain tops, and valleys. Ultimately, each leader shares how God made "A Way Outta No Way." Additionally, *The Heart of a Leader* is an opportunity to revisit your leadership, your gifts and your why to recenter and focus your true calling. Ultimately, each leader shares how God made "A Way Outta No Way."

Three questions, then I'm out!

First, the authors share their passion and their heart. As a leader, what breaks your heart? There are many problems and challenges in the world. What keeps you up at night? What tugs at your heart? Where can you make an impact? What areas have you experience success previously? Nehemiah found himself crying out to God. He was overwhelmed with the problems of the people. The weight on his heart was such a burden that he prayed and cried out to God for help!

Where can you make an impact? Social injustice, racial inequality, quality education, homelessness, racism, poverty, food insecurity, mental illness, or the like.

Secondly, the authors share their abilities. From nurses, educators, ministers, business professionals, entrepreneurs, and health care workers, each author has demonstrated great success in each of their areas. They each have distinctive abilities just as Nehemiah. What are your abilities? God blessed all of us with specific and unique talents. Seek wise counsel from other leaders. Be honest with yourself. God uses all people in incredible ways as evidenced in this wonderful work.

Lastly, what resources do you have? The authors narrate stories of scarcity and abundance. Times when they struggled financially, emotionally, in their health, in relationships, as well as with food and home security. But like Nehemiah, they also experienced abundance. What does your passion require? Time? Money? Support? Do you have enough, or do you need to seek assistance? Who can assist you?

The Heart of a Leader will inspire you and reignite your flame of purpose that is simmering within. Allow the authors to fan the flames! Get ready to reengage with your heart that will ultimately lead to purposeful and effective leadership.

Levatta Levels

Leader in Education & Executive Mentorship

Dr. Levatta L. Levels is a 30-year Veteran Educator in which she has been an Elementary Teacher, Assistant Principal, Principal, Bilingual Specialist, Director, Assistant Superintendent, and Superintendent.

Currently, Dr. Levels is the Chief Executive Officer of Higher Levels Educational Group,

Adjunct Professor, Author, Advocate, and Professional Mentor. As the CEO, Dr. Levels provides professional development and mentoring throughout the country.

For the inaugural implementation of the Delta Teacher Efficacy Campaign, Dr. Levels served as an Academy Facilitator, in which she served as an online instructor for the Teacher Efficacy Academy – TEA I and TEA II. She managed participants in the TEA-assigned region strengthening teacher effectiveness. She furthered her work with DTEC by collaborating with the Texas Team advocating for the implementation of the Every Student Succeed Act across the state.

Working with the Texas Education Agency, she provided training and mentoring to principals throughout the state of Texas over the last 10 years. Known for her "leadership abilities," she has worked with many schools towards improving student academic achievement and building principal leadership capacity.

Dr. Levels has served many professional and civic organizations, including Delegate to the Texas Democratic Convention representing Senate District 23, DeSoto Chamber of Commerce Board, Leadership Southwest Board, Big Brothers Big Sisters Southern Region Board, University of North Texas Exes Board, and the University of North Texas Advisory Council.

She is active with the Texas Association of School Administrators, National Council of Negro Women, Parent Teacher Association, UNT Trailblazers, Texas Counseling Association, Texas Association of Black School Educators, Delta Sigma Theta Sorority Incorporated, and the Zeta Eta Alumnae Association.

Dr. Levels earned an Ed.D. in Educational Leadership from Texas A&M University-

Dr. Levatta L. Dean Levels

Commerce. She earned both her Bachelor of Science and Master of Education with a focus on Education Administration from the University of North Texas and completed the Superintendent Certification program with the University of Houston-Victoria. She is most proud of her two children Leah and Lofton and granddaughter London.

The Heart of a Leader Leadership Lessons

_____

_____

_____

_____

_____

_____

_____

_____

_____

_____

_____

_____

_____

_____

_____

_____

_____

_____

_____

_____

_____

_____

_____

_____

_____

_____

_____

_____

_____

_____

_____

_____

_____

_____

_____

_____

_____

_____

_____

_____

_____

_____

_____

_____

_____

PREFACE

This project came at a pivotal time in my life where my leadership was questionable, and I decided to put all things on hold to pinpoint where I went wrong. To my surprise, I knew I had things I needed to address but when I assessed past situations, I realize I was not the only one who had things they needed to address and fix.

The heart of a leader is a body of work written to impact, provide real-time solutions, and give insight on leadership for novice, new, aspiring, and emerging leaders. Let's be clear at the onset, this book is not for everybody. We are not trying to reach everybody and as a leader, you must understand you will not reach everybody. Just reach those that you can and those in your sphere of influence.

This book is designed to be used as a resource guide, tool, and manual for new leaders that CEOs, trainers, directors, superintendents, principals, ministry leaders, governmental leaders, and health care officials employ, hire, consult, or train. The goal is to assist readers with building strong relationships among teams and groups to equip them to always lead well.

You will encounter leadership lessons from various women from various careers and business models who reside within the United States of America either in the state of Maryland or Mississippi. They share their words of wisdom, insight, experience, and strategies on leadership. Our foreword author hails from the great state of Texas so we have nicknamed this anthology "Maryland Meets Mississippi with a Spice of Texas."

There are a lot of smart and gifted leaders who do not know how to interact well with others. As a result, their leadership is not appreciated, and people look at them as harsh and insensitive people. The heart of a leader consists of having key characteristics where leaders value people and treat them as such and not like products or objects.

You will read chapters from women who lead in Marketplace Ministry, Health & Wellness, Entrepreneurship, Education & Executive Mentorship, Nursing, Nonprofits and Community Revitalization, as well as Corporate Leadership, Church Administration, Health, and Self Care.

If you need to, grab a pen and paper, an electronic note taking device, or simply open up your heart before you read so you can hear and receive lessons and tips that will forever change your effectiveness as a leader.

-Simene' Walden, Visionary of The Heart of a Leader

LESSONS FROM UNSUSPECTING LEADERS

The heart of a leader is one that understands you're only on earth for a set amount of time, and you must be intentional about completing the tasks you've been assigned. Ecclesiastes 9:10 declares, "Whatever your hand finds to do, do it with your might; for there is no work or device or knowledge or wisdom in the grave where you are going." So many times, I've found myself having amazing ideas but I just write them down and never pursue them or I'll say, "I'll get to it later."

Later is not a time that's promised. Leaders must take advantage of the time they are given and use that time wisely.

Robyn Conerly

W ho, me? I'm not a leader."

"Pick someone else."

I can't do it like they can."

These are statements I'm sure you've either said yourself or heard someone else say. I call these "statements from an unsuspecting leader." An unsuspecting leader is one who isn't aware that he or she is a leader. They assume leaders are those with a certain background or pedigree, those who have an important title, or those that don't look the way they look. Well, this is untrue. A leader is simply someone who has influence on another person. I'd like to share with you lessons I've learned on my journey of becoming the leader God wants me to be.

To have the heart of a leader, you must first realize you are a leader. You must realize the gift of leadership you've been given is bigger than you and has been placed inside of you to help someone else. If you influence your children, you, my friend, are a leader. If you influence your friends, you, my friend, are a leader. If you influence your coworkers, you, my friend, are a leader. If you have influenced or currently influence others, you, my friend, are a leader.

When I think of an unsuspecting leader, I'm reminded of the leader Gideon. In the Bible, our first introduction of Gideon is finding him hiding. He was hiding grain, because the Midianites, the bullies of the land at that time, would constantly attack Gideon's people and destroy all their crops. On what appears to be a normal day, the angel of the Lord visits him and calls him "a mighty man of God; a mighty warrior." I'm sure Gideon didn't feel as if he was any of these things, but God said otherwise. God used Gideon to defeat a mighty army. He began with a team of 32,000, and God decreased his army to a team of 300 men. From Gideon, we learn that sometimes as a leader you can do more with the little. If you're a leader and what you are leading seems small now, don't despise small beginnings. God can give you victory and prosperity with the little.

Another lesson we can learn from another unsuspecting leader is you weren't created to do it all on your own. You must delegate. Moses was used by God to deliver a team of millions from slavery and bondage. On the journey to the land God promised them, we encounter Moses leading the people. Exodus 18:13 says, "The next day Moses took his seat to serve as judge for the people, and they stood around him from morning till evening." The people came to Moses seeking God's will. The people also brought all their disputes to Moses, and he judged every case. Jethro, Moses' father-in law, gives him amazing advice. He told him "What you are doing is not good. You and these people who come to you will only wear yourselves out. The work is too heavy for you; you cannot handle it alone." As a leader after God's heart, it's pertinent that you use the help he sends so that you are not worn out from the assignment He has given you. If you don't have people yet that you can depend on, ask God to send you the help you need.

Another important lesson we learn from Moses is that who we are is enough for us to step into the leadership role God has for us. Yes, we are always learning and growing, but we cannot allow fear, inadequacies, or insecurities to stop us from saying yes to positions of leadership. Moses was given a great assignment from God, but he kept looking at himself. He kept looking at issues he thought disqualified him from being a great leader. As my pastor says, "We were not created to compete or compare but to contribute." You cannot compare yourself to other leaders, but you must walk boldly and confidently in who God created you to be. If you've felt a tug to say yes to a position of leadership but have allowed yourself to stand in the way— get out of your own way and take a leap of faith. The task may seem too big for you, or you may feel you don't have what it takes. We know God qualifies those he calls. If he's calling you to leadership, he will supply you with all you need. The heart of a leader is one that is open to receive constructive criticism that is aimed at seeing you grow.

Have you ever felt your leadership skills were becoming a little dull or in a sense outdated?

Well, *As iron sharpens iron, so one person sharpens another* according to Proverbs 27:17. We need people on our team who are going to keep us from becoming dull. *If the ax is dull, and one does not sharpen the edge, then he must use more strength*: based on Ecclesiastes 10:10. The more people we surround ourselves with who will not just tell us what we want to hear but need to hear, the sharper our gift of leadership will be.

The heart of a leader is one that understands you're only on earth for a set amount of time, and you must be intentional about completing the tasks you've been assigned. Ecclesiastes 9:10 declares, "Whatever your hand finds to do, do it with your might; for there is no work or device or knowledge or wisdom in the grave where you are going." So many times, I've found myself having amazing ideas but I just write them down and never pursue them or I'll say, "I'll get to it later." Later is not a time that's promised. Leaders must take advantage of the time they are given and use that time wisely.

The greatest example of a leader is Jesus!! He teaches us that the heart of a leader is the heart of a servant. You must have a heart for the people you lead. "Yet it shall not be so among you; but whoever desires to become great among you, let him be your servant," according to Matthew 20:26. Many times we can become so fixated on accomplishing goals that we neglect to really see and serve those on our team. Every person on the team is essential. Philippians 2:3-4 explicitly states, "Let nothing be done through selfish ambition or conceit, but in lowliness of mind let each esteem others better than himself. Let each of you look out not only for his own interests, but also for the interests of others." If we serve well, we will lead well.

Hey you! Yes, you! You are a leader, and you have an amazing opportunity to lead well. As we learn from unsuspecting leaders, we equip ourselves to be the best leaders we can be. We must know our worth, remain open to receive help, surround ourselves with those who will help sharpen our leadership skills, be intentional about getting our assignments completed, and serve the people we lead well.

Robyn Conerly

Leader in Entrepreneurship

Robyn Conerly is a Christian who loves God and loves serving His people. She is a member of Peter's Rock Family Worship Center COGIC under the illustrious leadership of Servant Leader - Pastor Joseph Hawkins.

She is a multi-faceted entrepreneur, innovator, educator, and change agent with a deep appreciation for ministering to others through a life committed to service. She is motivated by seeing others metamorphose from a place of darkness to one inundated with joy, hope, and faith.Robyn loves all things books and recently became a #1 bestselling author for the book Finally Free. She is also the owner of Losing 2 Win: an online wellness platform, tailoring life to meet people where they are. Clients are met with various options in maintaining optimal health, as Robyn is also a distributor of Omnitrition, a benefactor revolutionizing client's health and vitality.

Robyn is L.L.P.S. certified and believes in the power of our tailor-made, God-given voice. Her mission is to help others reclaim their voice, because we eat what we speak. She is the co-host of the virtual podcast, Shoot2Kill, along with her sister Pamela. In each episode, they shoot to kill negativity with the weapons of prayer, praise, and the Word of God and encourage others to do the same.

She is the co-founder of the non-profit 360 Degrees: Mind, Body, & Soul, a program that seeks to help others transition from one phase of life to another. Robyn desires to assist others in becoming all God has created them to be. She is also the co-owner of Biological Besties, with her sister, Pamela.

Robyn is the executive director and co-owner of PARC Academy and After School Program WPR, a nonprofit, virtual K-12 school developed due to the unforeseen events of the COVID-19 pandemic. Perhaps one of the best indicators of the awe-inspiring professional Robyn Conerly has been her unyielding contributions to the technological advancements provided to children during the pandemic. Together, along with her sister, Pamela, she has been able to provide both internet and technology (computers) to students ranging from grades K-12th attending school virtually. These ladies seek to encourage, motivate, champion, and inspire their students to be responsible, be resilient, and believe in themselves.

Robyn's appreciation for education isn't shown merely through her realms of service, but also in her person. She hosts a Bachelor of Science in Business Information Systems, a Master of Science in Instructional Technology, and is a certified teacher in both business and social studies.

Robyn's purpose is to be a community philanthropist who impacts lives through the giving of her time, talents, and treasure. She aspires to daily emanate the love of Christ and hopes others see Christ in her. Her ultimate goal is to fulfill her life's purpose while inspiring and uplifting others.

Email: robynconerly@yahoo.com

Facebook: Robyn Conerly

Instagram: @beyoutifulrobyn

Health and Wellness Business:

Omnitrition.com/losing2win

Book purchase: biologicalbesties.com/shop

YouTube Podcast: Shoot2Kill

The Heart of a Leader Leadership Lessons

_____

_____

_____

_____

_____

_____

_____

_____

_____

_____

_____

_____

_____

_____

_____

_____

_____

_____

_____

_____

_____

_____

_____

_____

_____

_____

_____

_____

_____

_____

_____

_____

_____

_____

_____

_____

_____

_____

_____

_____

_____

_____

_____

_____

_____

_____

Robyn Conerly

THE HEART OF A LEADER

*It is in reading and re-reading about the function and
definition of the physical heart that I approach the "heart" of
a leader. As I just mentioned, the heart is small in size but
controls the entire body. It is through the heart that we have
our life-giving source. Our blood is cleansed and sent
throughout our entire body and brings oxygen. Because of the
heart's major position of power in the physical body, we can
compare and see the major role that the heart of a leader has
on the body that he or she leads.*

Pamela Conerly

WebMD defines heart as "a muscular organ
about the size of a fist, located just behind
and slightly left of the breastbone. The heart
pumps blood through the network of arteries
and veins called the cardiovascular system. The
heart has four chambers. The right atrium
receives blood from the veins and pumps it to
the right ventricle. The right ventricle receives
blood from the right atrium and pumps it to the
lungs, where it is loaded with oxygen. The left

atrium receives oxygenated blood from the lungs and pumps it to the left ventricle. The left ventricle (the strongest chamber) pumps oxygen-rich blood to the rest of the body. The left ventricle's vigorous contractions create our blood pressure. The coronary arteries run along the surface of the heart and provide oxygen-rich blood to the heart muscle. A web of nerve tissue also runs through the heart, conducting the complex signals that govern contraction and relaxation.

It is in reading and re-reading about the function and definition of the physical heart that I approach the "heart" of a leader. As I just mentioned, the heart is small in size but controls the entire body. It is through the heart that we have our life-giving source. Our blood is cleansed and sent throughout our entire body and brings oxygen. Because of the heart's major position of power in the physical body, we can compare and see the major role that the heart of a leader has on the body that he or she leads.

The first two of the four chambers of the heart are the right atrium which receives the poor, deoxygenated blood and the right ventricle that pumps the blood out to the lungs where it will become oxygenated. Jesus Christ is the best living example of the heart of a leader! Jesus is the heart and as he walked through this world being 100% human and 100% God, He pulled in deoxygenated souls such as the disciples, other Christians, and you and me.

As we walk alongside of Him, work in ministry, and lead, we can become deoxygenated from the simple ins and outs of life. So, we must recycle our strength through the heart (Jesus) and become oxygenated or refilled by the Spirit of God again. As God cleanses and refills, us afresh, we essentially travel from the spiritual atrium to the spiritual ventricle where he sends us out to the lungs of life where we receive oxygen or the breath of God again.

Then, we are sent to the other side, also known as the left side or the last two chambers of the heart. The last two chambers of the physical heart are the left atrium which receives the rich, oxygenated blood and pumps it to the left ventricle. Then the left ventricle pumps the oxygen-rich blood to the rest of the body. After Jesus pulls in the poor, deoxygenated souls, He cleanses and washes us again. H refills us with his Spirit ("oxygen"). And finally, after we have been oxygenated again, He sends us out to help the entire body and to spread what he has placed inside of us to others in the body. What I gleam from Jesus being the heart are these 10 principles.

1) Try to lead like He led and do what He did. First, reach out to God when feelings of tiredness, exhaustion, pain, offense, and emptiness arise.

2) Ask Him to wash you afresh and forgive and cleanse you again with his blood as often as possible.

3) When leading, ask God to refill you with the Holy Spirit and to send you where you are predestined to go.

4) When leading, lead with the heart of God that will reach out to the lowest or dirtiest or most ostracized people. In other words, lead with compassion and a love and heart for people. Being a leader isn't anything if it isn't done in love.

5) When leading, lead with J.O.Y. in mind -- Jesus, Others, and then Yourself.

6) When leading, lead like Jesus and build those around you, use those around you, and refresh those around you.

7) When leading, lead like Jesus and lead in unity.

8) When leading, lead like Jesus and lead with the intent to help others become better.

9) When leading, lead like Jesus with a specific assignment in view.

10) When leading, lead like Jesus with a heart that connects with the heart of others.

Father God, I intercede for the heart of every leader that may read this book. Father, I pray that their individual hearts have been replaced with your heart of love, compassion, selflessness, servanthood, care, and concern. Father, refresh, renew, refill, heal the hearts of your leaders that may be depleted. Father, it is our sincere desire to serve, love, and lead like you. In Jesus name, Amen.

Pamela Conerly

Leader in Entrepreneurship

Pamela Conerly is the TV Host of Shoot2Kill, Executive Director, Entrepreneur, and a Certified Teacher. Pamela is an experienced business owner with over 18 years of experience and a demonstrated history of success in the education industry. Pamela has over 10 years of experience in Nonprofit Organization and For Profit Business Setups, Team Building, Staff Organization and Management, and Workshop Facilitation and Setup. Strong entrepreneurship professional.

https://www.facebook.com/conerly.pamela

https://www.linkedin.com/in/pamela-conerly-a9ba3961/

The Heart of a Leader Leadership Lessons

_____

_____

_____

_____

_____

_____

_____

_____

_____

_____

_____

_____

_____

_____

_____

_____

_____

_____

_____

_____

_____

_____

_____

THE HEART OF A LEADER

Humility is an important leadership trait. It is an effective tool for leading and motivating others, as well as stimulating productivity in a variety of leadership arenas. Humility, in its broadest sense, instills self-awareness, the appreciation of other people's strengths, being receptive to new ideas, and provides insight into personal self-performance. True humility requires courage and trust that stem from a leader's self-confidence and capabilities. True humility occurs when leaders consider the needs of their team as a priority. Selfless leaders are concerned with the success and needs of those that they lead.

Constance Woulard, RN, MSN

A n effective leader will make it a priority to help his or her people produce good results in two ways: making sure people know what their goals are and doing everything possible to support, encourage, and coach them to accomplish those goals. Your role as a leader is even more important than you might

45

imagine. You have the power to help people become winners." -Kenneth Blanchard

What are the essential traits of a good leader? What are the spiritual and intellectual components of the heart of a leader? What are the traits needed to make up the heart of a leader? Effective leaders must possess the traits and knowledge to develop and guide those which they lead to be their best self. The heart of a leader is one that is inclusive of humility, trust, servitude, authenticity, empathy, and integrity. Collectively, these traits form the foundation of the heart of a leader.

Humility is an important leadership trait. It is an effective tool for leading and motivating others, as well as stimulating productivity in a variety of leadership arenas. Humility, in its broadest sense, instills self-awareness, the appreciation of other people's strengths, being receptive to new ideas, and provides insight into personal self-performance. True humility requires courage and trust that stem from a leader's self-confidence and capabilities. True humility occurs when leaders consider the needs of their team as a priority. Selfless leaders are concerned with the success and needs of those that they lead. Leaders should focus on the well-being and success of those they lead, as well as their own personal well-being.

The heart of a leader embraces authenticity. Authentic leaders are aware of themselves as individuals and as a leader. Authentic leaders lead from a genuine stance and strive to bring out the best in those that they lead. They motivate and inspire trust and confidence within their team by providing a structure which promotes trust and harmony in the workplace. Collaboration and input from the team is important to leaders. Leaders must be able to maintain a sense of resilience when faced with adversity. Authentic leaders strive to develop honest and ethical relationships with those they lead.

Authenticity leads to and promotes trust in the leader-employee relationship. It is important that leaders are able to establish and promote trust among those that they lead. Trust is essential for the promotion of a harmonious work environment. Without trust, the leader is unable to maintain viable leader-employee relationships that are relevant and beneficial.

Integrity is present in various forms within the place. Ethical behavior and strong work ethic contributes to the character and traits of an effective leader. Leaders must embrace integrity as well as demonstrate behaviors of integrity while leading with a vision or purpose in mind. It is important to effectively communicate this vision or purpose to those they lead in order to successfully execute the leaders' organizational goals. Integrity of a leader fosters a therapeutic work environment and promotes ethical decision-making by the leader.

Having empathy as a leader promotes a caring environment in the workplace and instills trust in the leader by those of which they lead. Team members are more comfortable approaching the leader and maintaining open communication with the leader. Leaders must be able to empathize or "walk in the shoes" of those that they lead to fully understand them and to meet them where they are in their current station in life.

Servitude is a critical component or trait of the heart of a leader. Leaders must be flexible and step up to stand in the trenches with the team as needed. Servitude by the leaders, in many cases is simply a show of support to the team. This fosters respect among the team towards the leader and other team members.

Great leaders must possess a heart that embraces confidence, consistency, and clarity. They must be able to present and effectively communicate the goals and objectives of the organization. Leaders must have an emotional intelligence in order to be successful. Leaders must be willing to resist norms and stick to what is right for the team and the organization. Empathy, authenticity, compassion, servitude, and humility frame the heart of a true leader.

It is important that leaders motivate their team to empower them to be successful. This stimulates productivity in the workplace and various leadership arenas. Self-awareness of the leader and the appreciation of the strengths of the team instills confidence in the effectiveness of the team. At the same time, the heart of the leader helps them to realize they are unable to function alone and must be able to rely upon their team. The leader and the team must be able to coexist and function collaboratively. The true heart of a leader is one that inspires others to be their best and to professionally develop others towards future successes.

Constance Woulard is Divisional Nursing Director for Wellpath Recovery Solutions. In this role, she is accountable for nursing practice and quality across Wellpath Recovery Solutions, encompassing twelve sites within the United States, including Washington, Colorado, Alaska, Massachusetts, South Carolina, California, Texas, and Florida.

Ms. Woulard is a Best-Selling Author, Motivational Speaker, Transformational and Visionary Leader, and Nursing Educator. She is a nursing graduate coach for Instructional

Connections, Incorporated. She is the owner and founder of AWG Consulting, providing nursing consultative services to various healthcare agencies and long-term care facilities.

Ms. Woulard is a co-author of the Women Who Pray collaborative, igniting 90 days of prayer. The book was released on June 27, 2021. She is also a co-author of the Sister Leaders Anthology and the co-author of More Precious than Gems, She Knows Her Worth Anthology. She is dedicated to motivating and empowering others to be their best.

Ms. Woulard studied chemistry and English at the University of Southern Mississippi and earned a Bachelor of Science Degree. She later obtained certification in Secondary Education. She received a Bachelor of Science in Nursing from William Carey University and a Masters of Science in Nursing Education from William Carey University.

She is an esteemed member of Chi Eta Phi. Her nursing career has been dedicated to creating high quality, reliable systems of care and developing the next generation of nurses and health care professionals to lead in these ever-changing times.

Ms. Woulard was nominated by Becker's Healthcare Report as Healthcare Hero of 2020, Wellpath's Nursing Leader of 2020, and 100 Successful Women of the Gulf Coast to know in 2020.

https://www.facebook.com/constance.woulard.14

https://www.linkedin.com/in/constance-woulard-52478316/

The Heart of a Leader Leadership Lessons

_____

_____

_____

_____

_____

_____

_____

_____

_____

_____

_____

_____

_____

_____

_____

_____

_____

_____

_____

_____

_____

_____

_____

_____

_____

_____

_____

_____

_____

_____

_____

_____

_____

_____

_____

_____

_____

_____

_____

_____

_____

_____

_____

_____

_____

R.I.N.G-Leadership: Balancing on the Big Top

(Resilience, Integrity, Negotiation, and Governance)

You cannot be a truly effective leader while broken on the inside. The work may get done but you as a vessel will lack what is needed to complete the total and complete assignment. It is like someone who comes to a job interview, gets hired, and then shows up and looks from across the street at their new job saying, "I am going to enter one day." In leadership, when you are not healed and whole as an individual, there are gaping holes in your life that remain open because the work has not been done to move forward in whatever area that needs work.

Mavis A. Creagh

The familiar music blasts from the floor of the "Big Top" arena. People from all walks of life singing age old tunes. Everyone cheers

57

and laughs as the crowd bursts into uncontrollable enthusiasm. The atmosphere reminds you of the famous Ringley Brothers Circus.

Acrobats move with swift agility from ring to ring. Fire throwers displaying their natural abilities entertaining excited crowds. Lions roar from cages with wide-open frightful jaws. Beautiful women with fancy costumes and fine adornments smile, greeting guests at the entrance. Children run in with glee as their eyes light up walking into the huge vibrant atmosphere. People move back and forth, jumping up and down unable to control their excitement. Some yell with fear shocked by the loud noise, roaring lions, and entertainment. While others wait anxiously in hopes of the Ringleader appearing in the spotlight of the famous Big Top!

There is one person who has not made their appearance in the Big Top...The "Ringleader." In leadership, this could be looked at as your position. There can be much excitement; but at the end of the day how are you going to show up? Are you going to allow the noise to get you off track? I have been on both sides of the tent. I have been an entry level worker, a young child, and an unassuming participant of distractions. I have also been placed in positions of leadership as a mother, adult daughter, trusted friend, mentor, and executive. The good thing about being a leader is you are never too old or young to get in position. How you handle your placement, learn from your mistakes, and properly position your appointment will sustain and develop you both personally and professionally.

We have all been in different places in life. Many situations that appear to be smooth to some can be daunting to others. My highest accomplishment could be a stumbling block to a person who was not ready for the attention. One thing for sure in life and business if you do not make adequate preparation, it will show eventually. You cannot be distracted by the noise if you plan on moving forward. As a Ringmaster (Leader) of a circus must prepare for the performance (circus) in life and leadership, you must do the same.

What creates a great leader? Is it the company structure, strategic planning, support systems, demeanor, educational background, or simply personal determination? I think it is a combination of all these factors along with favor, timing, preparation, and grace.

You can be a leader in different aspects of life including business, family, or personally. One is not more important than the other however, I will discuss leadership in the nonprofit arena and community stabilization. I have worked with the same nonprofit for 14 years. I started out as temporary worker who was only supposed to work for 6 months. Well 6 months turned into years of ups and downs with tremendous learning curves. Through the process of favor and divine intervention, I became the Interim

Director 7 years ago. I have been serving as the Executive Director for over 4 years. This was not without struggles, heartaches, and hard seasons of development, growth, and leadership.

I have learned many things along my journey but one of the most important lessons learned is the personal work that is required to be a strong and sustainable leader. You can look good on the outside but eventually, if there is not self-work taking place, you will always end up in a deficit. One of the old sayings is, "You cannot pour from an empty well," This is my story times 100! Even recently, I was forced to regroup and put many things on pause in order to take care of myself. I believe this will prepare me for where I am headed moving forward in leadership and life. You cannot be a truly effective leader while broken on the inside. The work may get done but you as a vessel will lack what is needed to complete the total assignment. It is like someone who comes to a job interview, gets hired, and then shows up and looks from across the street at their new job saying, "I am going to enter one day." In leadership, when you are not healed and whole as an individual, there are gaping holes in your life that remain open because the work has not been done to move forward in whatever area that needs work.

Another aspect I have witnessed is when leaders allow external noise to create prolonged distractions. One of the women I know wanted to expand her business and create a sustainable brand. However, on numerous occasions she kept bringing up old issues with people and things that were beyond her control. I eventually told her that if she wanted to move forward as a leader, she needed to stop being distracted or would be at square one in a year.

One must remember in leadership there are often no winners or losers because the perspective of the position will turn a disheartening situation into a teachable and applicable tool for someone who is building a legacy. One of the strongest skills I have learned is to move with the punches. Every day will not be your winning season; however, do not throw in the towel. It is okay to vent and have frustrations, but you do yourself a disservice when you jump off the tight rope when the conditions become harsh or the audience in the **"Big Top"** turns. One of the hardest lessons I learned is to bet on yourself and even when you are doing your best someone in the crowd will boo (secretly or in public). You will never get everything right, but my foundation is the Creator whom I serve. Everyone is different and has their own views, but I know without a shadow of a doubt that the Most High has kept me. People will turn their backs on you when your performance is not what they expected or if others begin to sway the crowd. That is why it is important to know who and whose you are. My advice is to show up anyway, focus, and go forward with the plan regardless of who claps for you at the **Big Top**!

Another valuable lesson is to not mix feelings with business. **How you feel does not produce results.** This sounds harsh to some, but if I had to manage a business by my emotions, everyone would get cussed out at some point and I would end up on the 6 o'clock news! LOL...

There will always be an internal struggle wrestling for your attention and motivation. The main point is to have a fundamental awareness of your purpose realizing that anything and anyone meant to break your focus deserves no time or energy. Efforts may be off every now and then, but it becomes equivocal for true leaders to press pass the fanfare, hoopla, and distractors to the charges they were positioned to lead.

Some people have titles and accolades, but people will not follow their leadership. Often it is because they allowed the circus mentality to overthrow their perception. They may be too self-centered, arrogant, abrasive, unforgiving, or uncaring to lead others. When and if you find yourself in this posture, remember you can always reengage balance and turn down the noise (internally and externally) and regroup. If you have been living like a clown at the circus but are supposed to be a leader, you can take off the excessive makeup (living for applause, denying true purpose, pleasing others, etc.) and become a ***Ringleader*** in your Arena! The question I pose is, "How will you lead and what are you allowing to distract you from your focus?"

Remember, being a leader does not apply to one area of life. You are a leader for your family, job, business, or community. It is easy to excel highly in one arena and fail miserably at another if unchecked. My goal is to remind you that all areas matter and with clear focus, it is possible to lead in all areas of your life! My goal is to discuss leadership in business especially nonprofits and community. I would have never imaged 14 years ago starting a 6-month temporary position as a case worker only to end up becoming an Executive Director for the same nonprofit agency.

Some key aspects to leading in the nonprofit arena and community include true **"R.I.N.G. Leadership"**: *Resilience, Integrity, Negotiation, and Governance.*

Resilience: One of the most important factors in leadership beyond faith is being able to maneuver difficult situations. As the Executive Director of a nonprofit, it has not always been an easy road. When I first assumed the position of Interim Director, it was out of default. Our agency was in a dry season and many of those who stood by the bustling business before did not want to be associated in this season. Remember seasons of plenty and lack are biblical and business can experience these cycles. I remember people telling me I was crazy for staying and that I should jump to another nonprofit since I had enough experience. I was not persuaded, and I remembered what was promised to me by the Creator.

Now if you are in a business and have not been given clearance to release your duties, then it would be my strong suggestion to focus and get to work. You cannot worry about other's opinions and how they feel. But you must be willing to roll up your sleeves and produce a harvest. Some of us are so busy complaining that we forget that faith without works is dead. I can talk all day about what I want to happen, how there are not enough resources (nonprofits that is common...get creative), or what should be done. However, this does not yield results and as I stated earlier, how I feel does not produce results.

As a leader, remember to work unto the Creator and do not let external situations determine your production. You cannot afford to give up or give in on your business, especially a nonprofit. It is ok to take a break as needed;

but giving up cannot be an option. Recently, I wanted to give up on business, nonprofits, and new ventures. Today I dusted myself off, began a new business venture, started a new program that will positively impact lives, focused, and created a different mental perspective. It is ok to take rest but do not allow the situations to break your fortitude and fight. If you need additional help personally to perform professionally, there is no shame in that. It is better to be resilient and seek help from counsel, therapists, or the like than to completely shut down and not be able to move forward at all. Remember, although business is bank, if you are unable to function properly personally, it really does not matter. ***You are the most important priority in leadership. Take care of others but remember there is only one you and you cannot be replaced!***

Integrity: Your word and reputation will take you further than any degree or title. When trying to climb the ladder of success and interfacing with people, it is better to be integral than deemed successful. Some of the most successful people have fallen because they lacked integrity. Money and accolades will come if you operate in purpose and do it for the glory of the Most High. If you must lie, cheat, steal, back bite, or "throw someone under the bus," then the price is too high. Stay out of conversations that do not concern you and everything that you know does not need to be repeated. Separate yourself from foolishness, mess, and confusion. Everything that is said or done has the possibility to get back to someone. If you have a personal issue with someone that will not affect your business, keep it to yourself. You, my friend, may not be the easiest pill to swallow. We forget sometimes that grace has been given to us more than a few times.

I say that there are no perfect people, but those who are perfectly positioned! Even if you have not operated in integrity on a regular basis before, there is always room for change and the

Creator can make anything positive out of a negative situation. Some people get into dilemmas because they act out of desperation and want a solution right away. This, however, can have detrimental consequences and life altering affects. Some of us are not willing to suffer even a little bit to get to the next blessing. Trouble does not last forever, and we all have been tempted to do or say something that would take away from our integrity. Remember, every action has a reaction in business and in life.

3 Takeaways:

Do What is Right Even When Nobody is Watching.

Keep Your Mouth Off of People That Do Not Concern Your Business.

Do not Get Distracted in the Big Top!

Negotiations: Working to rebuild communities has been my focus for the last 14+ years in varying capacities. Whatever your position as a leader, remember there is no "I" in TEAM.

Most projects and programs in nonprofits and community development are funded by multiple sources. This means that even if you have a vision and plan, there is still a need to coordinate with multiple entities. If you have a mindset that "I can do it all by myself," then you need to hit the lottery. Even then, you would need someone to correctly implement the programs created. If you were over all the resources and did not have to answer to anyone, then perhaps you could take that approach, however, negotiations are necessary for success with nonprofits.

Negotiations can be internal or external. Each situation will have to be handled differently; but the goal is to remain focused on the mission and not become engulfed with distractions in the "Big Top." One of the best lessons I learned in a dry season was to tune out the naysayers and not be so quick to react when situations did not go my way. Some opportunities that I believed our company should have received fell through. But, in many situations, I had to negotiate with some of the same people who disappointed me. As a leader you must be humble and remember that every battle does not have to be met head on. Yes, you should stand up for yourself and not allow others to run over you. However, sometimes your best asset is that you see situations in the "Big Top" for what they are and continue to complete your role as a leader. "Pick and Choose Your Battles" because everyone is not your enemy and everyone that smiles in your face is not an ally. Remember to **Focus, Work, and Negotiate** for the *"Greater Good"* of the True Mission. Everything else at the end of the day is not important.

Governance: Nonprofits and Community Revitalization rely heavily on donated funds and grants. To monitor and maintain adequate responsibility, proper governance must be considered. As a leader in the nonprofit sector, it is always important to remember that you are not your own boss and are accountable to the Board of Directors. The Board has a fiduciary responsibility that the company is operating in accordance with their mission and functions with integrity as an agency. If you are in a leadership position in a nonprofit or want to start a nonprofit, remember resources (financial and in kind) must be accounted for. Before accepting any support monetarily or otherwise, always get a clear understanding in writing on the expectations and requirements.

Engage with any partners who have agreed to support the mission. Be willing to answer additional questions along the way as you operate programs and monitor resource opportunities. If anything is unclear about the required regulations, ask questions.

Another key aspect of leadership is to maintain proper records and stay audit ready. At any time, a nonprofit can be audited by external sources who provide financial and/or in-kind donations. Sometimes I have been asked why I did not go after certain opportunities, and it was because I was unsure if we had the ability at that time to adequately monitor and facilitate the program. It is better to be safe than sorry and you as a leader do not want to build a reputation of not being able to properly maintain donated resources.

Leadership overall is based on relationships and honesty. Honesty with yourself and honesty with others. It is easy to get distracted in the "Big Top" of Life and Leadership but remain focused even when the crowd is high! If you are a leader or aspiring leader, remember that your decisions carry more weight than someone else's. It is like a domino effect that can turn into a real circus if you are not careful.

Be the **R.I.N.G. Leader** and not the clown of the Big Top! Your legacy as a leader is constantly at stake. In the spotlight and behind the scenes leaders must still be accountable and adaptable for what is best for the business. Each time I transitioned into a new position I made it a point to learn who else had a similar mission, engage their similar visions, support as available, and most importantly build real relationships.

Community development requires relationships: relationships build partnerships, partnerships build trust, trust garners resources, resources support productivity, and productivity produces ongoing sustainability.

Resilience, Integrity, Negotiation, and Governance build a solid foundation to grow businesses and communities. It is like a fine balancing act that takes place on the "Big Top." As a leader it is essential to evaluate and take inventory on a regular basis to see if you are acting as the crowd or a true *Leader*!

Leading properly takes work, perseverance, and faith but with clear direction and guidance any circus can be *MASTERED* by the right *R.I.N.G LEADER*!

Mavis A. Creagh.

Leader in Nonprofits and Community Revitalization

Mavis A. Creagh is a Best-Selling Author, Speaker, Consultant, Women's Advocate, Entrepreneurial Strategist, Columnist, and Online Show Host. She currently serves as the Executive Director of R3SM, Inc. (Recover, Rebuild, and Restore Southeast MS) a nonprofit founded following Hurricane Katrina. Recently, she established Mavis A. Creagh Consulting, LLC, a brand that offers editing, writing, speaking, and business consultation along with We Women Ministries, Inc. a ministry created to empower, enrich, and elevate women from all backgrounds. She has an extensive knowledge of recovery following natural disasters with a foundation in revitalization of communities, philanthropy, and economic development.

Over the past four years, Mavis provided oversight of 30 new constructions, 100+ repair projects, and over 5 million dollars in volunteer labor and donations throughout the State of Mississippi. Through her leadership, R3SM, Inc. now owns and operates the fully renovated historic 10,000 sq. ft. Volunteer House formally known as the "Robinson Inn" located in the Historic Newman Buschman Neighborhood. R3SM's "Robinson Inn" is a true community asset that offers administrative offices, a small event venue, training space, temporary and transitional housing, seasonal University lodging, and accommodations for up to 60 volunteers! One of her proudest accomplishments is her teenage son, Jordan! He is a phenomenal creative, chef, and upcoming business owner.

Adding to her strong portfolio of success, writing is yet another way she serves the world. Proven to be a prolific writer, Mavis will release her first solo project, a Women's Devotional later this year! Mavis is an advocate for change and serves on the following Boards: NAMI MS (National Alliance of Mental Illness), NAMI Pine Belt, Mississippi VOAD (Volunteer Organizations Active in Disaster), Pine Belt Veterans Task Force, Purple Heart Homes Pine Belt Mississippi, along with additional Community Advisory Boards.

Mavis A. Creagh Consulting

www.mavisacreagh.com

Facebook, Instagram, LinkedIn: Mavis A. Creagh

The Heart of a Leader Leadership Lessons

_____

_____

_____

_____

_____

_____

_____

_____

_____

_____

_____

_____

_____

_____

_____

_____

_____

_____

_____

Mavis A. Creagh

CONNECT WITH THE LEADER WITHIN AND EMBRACE YOUR INNER LEADERSHIP SKILLS

I am here to reconfirm and affirm that most of the leadership skills that we need to be successful and become effective leaders are already born within us. We are more than capable of perfecting them with time and true intentions. No longer question if you are built for the role of a leader, but know that you are a leader in your own right. Confidently step into the role without arrogance: in whatever capacity of your life that it is required of you with an open mind in order to grow and assist others while they grow with you through the process.

Janael Palmer

We are all capable on some level to be leaders in our own rights. We lose sight or are not aware of this possibility because we do it naturally without associating what we are doing with any particular skill, or we may just see what we are doing as survival or something that just needs to be done. We have to understand who we are, what it means to be in a leadership role, and how we function in that role as the leader. Never take for granted that we have all the tools within us that we need to effectively handle any role in our lives that we take on as leader or the head. We will not focus our time on trying to understand poor and ineffective leadership skills because I am sure that at some point in our lives, we have all been under the leadership of someone was or did the total opposite of all that we have identified as great leadership traits and skills.

This chapter is focused on building or rebuilding the confidence within yourself for novice leaders or leaders who know that they should be in leadership but continue to question whether they are capable or not. After reading this chapter the goal is that you would no longer question your capabilities as a leader, but instead embrace and cultivate the skills that you know you already have to become an outstanding and affective leader. Before we get to into depth with discussing what makes us leaders in our own rights, let's begin the conversation by me first introducing who I am and define what is leadership and how is it displayed in our day-to-day endeavors.

Who Is Janael Palmer?

Janael Palmer is a 34-year-old woman who was born in Sierra Leone, West Africa, and the mother of two amazing boys. She came to the United States at the age of six and lived with her mother and late father in Maryland, where she spent the majority of her life. Janael is a lover of life, people, and is determined to lead a life of purpose and servitude. By profession, Janael holds the title of Adult-Gerontology Nurse Practitioner and is currently working at the nursing bedside as a Registered Nurse in order to be impactful in the lives of the patients that she cares for. Janael is an aspiring entrepreneur who is working on a few business ventures.

Along with her professional titles, she is a woman that wears many hats or other titles in both her personal and professional life. The most meaningful title amongst all the titles is that of a mother. This is a role that she takes great pride in to make sure that she is leading her children by example in the ways that they should go. Titles do not or should not define who a person is, so it is always important to understand individuals beyond their title to truly determine their leadership style and capabilities as a leader.

I have always known within myself that I would make an awesome leader in any area that I choose to take accountability as the leader or head of the project. Growing up, I naturally knew that I would be affective in roles of leadership due to my confidence, outgoing personality, and the ability that I had to positively influence and encourage others to be their best selves. In various projects that I have been involved in, when I am much focused on it or dedicated to it, I loved taking on the role of the organizer or what may be considered the leader in order to work with others to get the job done. As we grow older, sometimes life begins to happen, and we start getting involved in situations that may not be ideal for who we are or who we want to be. This is especially true in early adulthood, and we may not always know how to handle such situations. It has the potential to take a toll on us and affect us in ways we never even imagined. As I took time to reflect as I am older now, I realize that some of these life experiences may have occurred as a designed plan for our greater good. At times, it may not seem that it is designed for the greater good, so it can cause one to lack confidence, question their own capabilities, and make one deem their light so that the spotlight doesn't shine out of fear of having to take ownership of life circumstances that may have been too traumatic for us to process or that we just cannot seem to forgive ourselves for.

Now, this has been my experience, and I allowed things that happened in my life that sometimes were beyond my control to cause me to neglect and ignore my inner leadership tendencies. When I started learning to let go of things, I could not control and take ownership of things that I could control, I was able to understand myself more. I started taking baby steps to start connecting back to the purpose that lived within me. One to lead myself, my family, my children, my friends, and others within my professional life and to push us to achieve more.

I am here to reconfirm and affirm that most of the leadership skills that we need to be successful and become effective leaders are already born within us. We are more than capable of perfecting them with time and true intentions. No longer question if you are built for the role of a leader, but know that you are a leader in your own right. Confidently step into the role without arrogance: in whatever capacity of your life that it is required of you with an open mind in order to grow and assist others while they grow with you through the process.

No longer allow yourself or your inner negative critic to hinder or cripple you from what God has already equipped you for. Spend time connecting with yourself on deeper levels and embrace your inner leader. It is deep within you and ready to shine for the good of all under your leadership including yourself.

What Is a Leader and How Do We Determine Who Is Capable of Leadership Role?

Let me start by saying that a leadership role is a calling on our life in which we are ordained the responsibility of guiding others in order to get things accomplished. We should not take this role lightly and be open to committing to continued learning. This may include participating in workshops, classes, and collaborating with others that can continue to fuel growth in our leadership abilities and skills.

A leader is someone that has a vision to improve things for the better and use their leadership to assist with change. Leadership is not about titles, salary, or specific characteristics, but it's an art of having the right attitude, skills, techniques, and developed intuition to drive and motivate individuals to work towards achieving a common goal because of choice. All leaders do not lead in the same way, and they do not have the same life experiences. This allows each leader to be unique in their own right. The leader can also be known as the person in charge of operations to help guide and make important decisions in order to keep operations going.

Leaders tend to possess certain characteristics and qualities that help them become effective in their role as a leader. Leadership can be good or bad based on the intentions of the leader and the approach in which they choose to lead in. Effective leadership is what we consider good leadership, and it is governed by important leadership traits. Some include self-awareness, integrity, influence, empathy, being strong, becoming good listeners, courageous, respectable, their ability to delegate, their creativity, positivity, gratitude, communication skills, learning agility, their ability to be constructive in their criticism of their team, as well as the finesse to bring out the leadership in others.

We also must understand that leadership is not about being the boss, but it's about sharing in the responsibilities. A good leader takes accountability for the team's efforts whether they are successful, or the goal set to achieve is not accomplished. Leaders are willing to reevaluate with their team ways to improve in order to achieve different outcomes. When we usually think of leadership, some automatically associate them with work life or business life, but we can be leaders in both our personal and professional life.

As stated earlier, the role of leadership can be exercised in any area of your life; for example, as a mom I am the leader to my children. I have influence over them, and I choose to influence in positive ways. As a nurse,

I have a leadership role in the lives of my patients, so I choose to care for them to the best of my ability and to effectively educate them on maintaining better health.

Leadership has different styles, and I am a firm believer that no one style of leadership works always. I personal believe that there may be a need to mix leadership styles in order to accomplish the overall outcome of the greater goal. It is important that the leader understands their role as the leader.

The role of the leader is to provide the team with a vision, establish a plan to execute the vision, create an organizational structure, determine effective ways of communication, set a deadline for the vision to be completed, empower the team by delegating specific tasks to be completed by each individual, influence the team by motivating them to complete the job, and then manage their own time wisely as the leader to attend to bigger operations that move the vision forward.

Leadership styles are used as a form of grouping how individuals in the positions of leadership conduct themselves as they take on the responsibility of leading others. The leadership styles that we are familiar with are autocratic, democratic, laissez-faire, and paternalistic. Autocratic or authoritarian leadership style is like a dictatorship that focuses on command and control. Under such leadership, those being lead are given clear expectations on what needs to be done, the time frame in which it should be done, and the exact way that it should be done. In this type of leadership there is not much room to be creative due to the strict guidelines that needs to be meet. In the democratic or participative leadership style, those under this leadership have a voice or contribute to how things should be run. In the democratic leadership style, guidance is offered to the members but everyone has an equal voice and are leaders in their own right, and although in this type of leadership the leader makes the final decision on how things should operate, they still take into consideration the suggestions of the others. In my personal opinion, this is the most effective leadership style. Take time to briefly evaluate each leadership style and understand what it means to be that style of leader. Laissez-faire, or delegative leadership style, on the other hand, has no form of guidelines or leadership being represented and in therefore the members involved under such leadership are left to make decisions on their own. Laissez-faire leadership roles are not clearly defined and this lack of clarity tends to leave the members unmotivated to accomplish things. On the other hand, this style may work when the leader is leading a group of experts that are already familiar with their roles and what they bring to the project. Last but not least, we have the paternalistic or the matriarch or patriarch style of leadership, which is when you have a leader that has taken on a role of a dominant authority figure and treats the members as an extended family. Under this form of leadership, the leadership the leader treats everyone like family and expects from them trust, obedience, and loyalty. In this form of leadership, the leader always considers the greater good of the "family" members and makes decisions based on that greater good. Another characteristic of this type of leader is that they put emphasis on the importance's of members being educated and socially informed, so they heavily invest in opportunities that will allow members to improve their business and interpersonal skills. If this type of leadership is used properly, members attached to it tend to work harder to reach or exceed their tasks in a timely manner in order to please the leader. Another thing to also consider in this leadership style is the possibility of the leader "parent figure" upsetting the members or family structure in a crisis, or is deemed to be unfair and have favorites, this can be a cause of confusion and resentment, which in turn will destroy that bond of trust, obedience, and loyalty.

After understanding the different leadership styles and also understanding who you are, which leadership style you are used to based on your own life experiences—whether it be in your personal and professional past—determine which leadership style resonates most based on who you are and your life experiences. Also, assess the pros and cons of the leadership styles that you have personally experienced and determine which elements were affective and which ones were not as you make your decision on how you should lead in your own right. However, also do not forget to assess the individuals you may be leading and which leadership styles may be effective for them as well. Balance is best found in taking the positives of each leadership style and working to better improve it daily in your own way.

Remaining an Effective Leader:

I am glad to have been able to clear up any confusion, lack of confidence or doubt that you may have had in your mind as a new or immerging leader, so now let's discuss the role of maintaining good leadership.

The beginning of remaining an effective leader is adhering to the positive characteristics and traits that make an effective leader. Develop a checks and balance system that your team and you can use to maintain and hold each other accountable while living authentically and effectively. Just like you are able to give your team constructive criticism, always be open to allow your team to also constructively criticize your leadership skills. Be open for change as necessary while continually meeting the needs of your team. Always put your team in a position to lead in their own right. Allow them to take on leadership roles and work with them to develop the leadership skills that they also possess. Be aware that none of us have all the answers so be willing to seek out answers to things you do not know. Be honest with yourself in regard to your strengths and areas of weakness. Acknowledge that it may require more work to strengthen those areas. Always do what is in the best interest of your team and your leadership should never be based on personal gain. Remaining an effective leader will cause you to want to be forward in your thinking and progression. Stagnation will cause your leadership to decrease in its effectiveness.

After reading this chapter, I am convinced you have determined that in order to be an Effective Novice or Emerging Leader, you have to be able to confidently connect and trust the inner leader within yourself. You have to understand what a leader is, what it means to be in leadership, the characteristics of an effective leader, understand leadership styles, understand the role of the leader, and be able to maintain effective leadership.

From my experience with leadership, it is not an easy road nor is it a straightforward path. However, regardless of your area of leadership expertise, you will experience both good and bad outcomes. It is still important to acknowledge a starting and end point to the common goal. As leaders, we have to be open to flexibility, be able to make hard decisions, self-reflect, and continue personal and professional development. Leaders must know when it may be time for a break to pour into self and to gain some mental clarity in order to continuously lead effectively.

Remember that our success starts and ends with us so whenever in doubt, don't hesitant to stop and take the time to connect within yourself to gain the strength that you need to push forward. Lead from the heart with compassion and empathy, but also never leave your mind and experiences behind as you lead in truth.

Janael Palmer

Janael Palmer

Leader in Health and Wellness

Janael Palmer is thirty-four and she was born in Sierra Leone, West Africa. She is a daughter, mother, someone's significant other, a sister, and a loyal friend. She is a beautiful soul inside and out. She enjoys long walks on the beach, shopping, and spending time with family. She is a lover of people and enjoys helping other women as well as herself spend more time loving on themselves.

Janael is a Geriatric Nurse Practitioner, who is currently working as a Registered Nurse. She is a Health and Wellness Coach that assists moms with making more time to enjoy selfish moments to focus on their self-care, mental, and emotional health.

Check out her children's book she published with her two young sons: Nubian Dynasty. Nubian Dynasty covers 12 principles that help restore royalty to the black family. It reiterates that Black History which is rooted in African History is not something to just be celebrated once a year in February, but it is a yearlong commitment to the Black Family Unit. Nubian Dynasty educates, empowers, and elevates readers in understanding that we are strong, resilient, and a powerful source of life and Hope.

https://www.instagram.com/janaelpalmer/

https://www.facebook.com/originalafricanroyalty/

The Heart of a Leader Leadership Lessons

_____

_____

_____

_____

_____

_____

_____

_____

_____

_____

_____

_____

_____

_____

_____

_____

_____

_____

_____

_____

_____

_____

KEEP THE FAITH

It's true when the enemy comes in like a flood, God will lift a standard against him. But you must SPEAK THE WORD and BOLDLY DECLARE IT IN FAITH. Let the word do the work. Don't become fearful and begin speaking what the media says. Resist speaking what the world system says. Speak the word over your situation and let God intervene. With God, we win every day in every way. Don't stress over things you cannot control. Rest assured, God hears your prayers and He will deliver on time. There's nothing like God's Timing. I've learned when things are spiraling out of control, God is strategically rearranging things in order. Oftentimes he will even allow chaos in our lives to propel us to our destiny.

Tammie T. Tubbs

One of the hardest things to do as a leader is to lead with a broken and wounded spirit. As crazy as it may sound, oftentimes individuals are unaware and cannot distinguish whether they are broken or not within. Unfortunately, some are blinded to the reality that life has wounded them, and their actions are affecting others. Regardless of how one may try to camouflage the tone of your voice, negative words, and body language will definitely tell the story in one way or another. Yes, broken crayons can still color, but they don't color the same. With that being said, when you are wounded as a leader, negativity, bitterness, and the tendency of being sarcastic is evident.

How do I know you may ask? I was once broken, battered, bruised while pretending as if I was A-okay and in reality, I was miserable and causing pain to those in my circle. Crying myself to sleep while perfecting the face that led others to believe I was healed, yet my spirit was wounded. In this chapter I share my heart and encourage you to Keep the Faith while healing from within. As leaders we must "keep the faith" because someone's life is depending on you to overcome.

Ever felt like giving up? Throwing in the towel? Battled Depression? Committing Suicide? Or maybe walking away from God? I'll be honest and say those were my thoughts once upon a time. But by the grace of God I'm still alive and prospering in all areas of my life. Throughout my 43 years of living, the lyrics I had to learn was how to trust him and to take him at his word. They have become a true revelation to me. Although God commands us in Deuteronomy 31:6 to be of good courage, often times it's not as easy as it seems to keep the faith. When walking by faith one may feel lost as if they are about to fall face first, but just in the nick of time, God always steps in and does, exceeding abundantly above all we could ask or think concerning the matters of our heart. **Ephesians 3:20.**

Some lose faith when the breakthrough miracles do not manifest instantly. Many become discouraged, depressed, perplexed, and allow bitterness to seep in. Even when

Moses was discouraged (scared, losing faith) God had to remind him that I will be with you; I AM THAT I AM. As a matter of fact, he tells him I am the LORD 5 times in Exodus: 6:2, 6:6, 6:7, 6:8, 6:29. Just as God reminded Moses, we too should refresh our memory of who God is and remember the countless victories he's won on our behalf. If your faith tank is low today, be encouraged. God will never leave you nor forsake you (Hebrews 13: 5-6). Keep the Faith!

Walking by Faith is never easy especially when your natural mind can't perceive what the spirit is saying. Although Abraham trusted God, I'm sure he can attest to the fact that the journey wasn't easy. I can hear him saying there was turbulence, stumbling blocks, doubts, fears, and anxiety along the way but I had a word from the Lord.

Understand the assignment of the thief is to steal, kill, and destroy according to John 10:10. His ultimate goal is to bring doubt and unbelief to get us to waver in trusting the promises of God. But as believers, we must hold on to the word of God and keep the faith. The enemy desires that we focus more on our circumstances than the word of God. He wants us to worry about the economy rather than praise God who has the whole world in his hands. It's true when the enemy comes in like a flood, God will lift a standard against him. But you must SPEAK THE WORD and BOLDLY DECLARE IT IN FAITH. Let the word do the work. Don't become fearful and began speaking what the media says. Resist speaking what the world system says. Speak the word over your situation and let God intervene. With God, we win every day in every way. Don't stress over things you cannot control. Rest assured, God hears your prayers and He will deliver on time. There's nothing like God's Timing. I've learned when things are spiraling out of control, God is strategically rearranging things in order. Often times he will even allow chaos in our lives to propel us to our destiny.

I'm reminded of one of the most devastating times in my life, when I almost lost my mind, my faith, and walked away from God. November 17, 2004, and January 29, 2005: two of my sons Terrance and Tyler passed away within 2 months of one another from the #1 Genetic killer for children under the age of 2: spinal muscular atrophy. During this time, I resided in North Carolina, 13 hours away from my Mississippi family. I was lost, depressed, and could not understand for the life of me WHY would God allow this to happen. My sons could not sit up, walk, or crawl, nor did they have head control. All I could remember saying was WHY God? Why Me?? I felt defeated and alone. For a while, I didn't want to attend church or even hear anyone mention faith because I was angry. But I soon learned God had a plan and purpose for it all. Although I didn't understand the process then, in hindsight I understand now more than ever He was refining me, pruning me, and healing me to be a living testament of his healing power. Praise

Be To God I have a sound renewed mind and I have been made whole by the power of the Holy Spirit. Believe me it was a not a quick fix, but I had to follow the acronym God gave me to overcome death and depression to keep the faith. In obedience, I share with you.

1. **K**ill your Flesh. In order to keep the faith we must die daily to our flesh. I believe **Romans 8:3-7** explains it best. Our egos, sinful nature, and pride must die so we can become more spiritually minded than carnally minded. In order to Grow in Christ, some things have to go in Jesus Name.

2. **E**xercise your faith. Without faith it is impossible to please God. In other words, if you are believing God in a certain area, do what you can in the natural and he will add the super to the natural you are believing for. Give him something to work with. Don't Delay! Apply for the job, the home loan, the car

loan, prepare the baby nursery, or set the table for your Boaz. Remember with God, all things are possible. **Matthew 19:23-30**

3. Expect God to move SUDDENLY in your life. It's not uncommon for God to do anything suddenly for his people. Ask Hezekiah in **2 Chronicles 29:36 and Isaiah 48:3.** If you can BELIEVE it, he will Perform it. Prepare. Get in Expectancy Mode! As a matter of fact, say this with me, I EXPECT GOD TO MOVE FOR ME TODAY! Now Praise Him. It is So! and So IT IS!

4. Praise him in advance. Don't wait until you see the miracle breakthrough. Begin to reference him with adoration and praise. Remember when the Praises God up, the Blesser comes down to shower blessings. Send up a Judah Praise and Watch God shift the atmosphere in your

favor. Let everything that has breathe Praise Ye the Lord. **Psalm 150:6**

5. **T**rust God. You have tried it your way. Why not Trust the plan and purpose God has for your life? Trust in the Lord with all thine heart and lean not to thy own understanding, in all thy ways, acknowledge him and he shall direct thy path. **Proverbs 3:5-6** Trusting God saves you a lot of time, energy and money. He always knows what's best for you.

6. **H**elping Others in Need. One the greatest blessings is to help someone along the way while you are going through a fiery trial faith walk. I've learned while I'm caring for others, God is behind the scene favoring me because I moved out of the way and shifted my focus to assist someone else rather than worry about my own issues. Hebrews 13:16 (Sharing Pleases God).

7. Enough is Enough. If you desire to keep the faith you must rebuke the devil and all his imps. Take authority over your family, home, ministry, finances, and life by speaking the word of God. If you are sick and tired of being sick, then this stage should be easy. James 4:7 clearly states, "Submit yourselves therefore to God, Resist the devil, and he will flee from you."

8. Fast and Pray. If you are believing for a healing, deliverance, or just need God to move in your situation, I highly recommend setting aside time with him to meditate and seek His heart. Some things only come by fasting and praying. Read **Mark 9:28-29 and Matthew 17:1-21.** Believe me, the sacrifice of turning my plate over was well worth it. Pray without ceasing. Simply talk to Him like you talk to your friends but instead of

gossiping, pray the word and remind God of His promises.

9. Acknowledge God as your Shepherd. **Psalm 23** declares the Lord is my Shepherd, I shall not want. If He is your shepherd, God will lead and guide you into all truths. With Him as your leader (Lord of your Life) your faith walk will get stronger daily as you seek Him through the word of God. Yield your will to God and follow His voice.

10. Inner Peace: Drown out the noise, turn the television off, turn the world off, and tap into inner peace. Often times I would hear my grandmother say, "There's nothing like a peace of mind." During this pandemic I personally learned how to stay in peace by exercising, journaling, walking, singing, painting, organizing, and yes listening to music and reading the word of God. Pampering yourself works for sure. A

piece of wisdom from my heart is you may want to alleviate friends or family in your life who add confusion and/or drama to your life. Ask yourself, how do you feel when they leave your presence? Empowered or Defeated. **Philippians 4:7**

11. Testify-If God has been good to you, say YEA! Rehearse previous victories He has won. Reflect on the times when God made a way out of no way. Write down the moments when he touched someone's heart to bless you. Think on the "If it had not been for the Lord on my side, where would I be?" Think on "If he did it before, he will do it again." Open your mouth and share what the Lord God has done for you. **Revelation 12:11.**

12. Hold on. Help is on the Way. Even when times are unbearable and there seems to be no way of escape, hold on and keep the faith. Help is on the way. God will most

definitely provide a ram in the bush. We must follow Abraham's example lifting our eyes to the father as Jehovah Jireh, our provider. Genesis 22:13

My Personal Keeping the Faith Testimony

Looking back, all I had was **Faith** when I returned home to Mississippi after nearly 15 years to begin television ministry. I vividly remember pulling up to my aunt Daisy's (Cal) home in my Nissan Maxima with tears in my eyes saying, "Ok God, I'm here. If it's your will, it's your bill. I have returned to this place called **There**. I believe you have commanded your people to sow NS feed me so my television ministry will grow and you will get the glory out of it. To God Be the Glory, 10 years later, I am thriving and prospering on television. I am debt free on the Christian Television Network WEPH TV 49, On Point Network, MaxxSouth Broadbrand, Apple TV, Cable One, Comcast, Dish Network, ROKU, Amazon, Apple TV, and OnPointe Network.

In addition, God has favored me to publish five books: I Still Have Joy, Woman II Woman: Will The Real You Please Stand You?, I Survived Death, Depression and Divorce, and I published an insert of my life journey in Testimonies of Trials & Triumphs authored by Tiffany Miller Harris. It's been a faith journey, yet I am still trusting him for greater during this pandemic.

Don't lose faith my friend. Keep the Faith! It's your time and your season to prosper and walk in your divine destiny.

Blessings and Favor.

Favor is upon you. Giving up is not an option. Keep the Faith.

Tammie Tubbs

Leader in Health and Self Care

Tammie Tubbs resides in Starkville, Mississippi, where she serves an Evangelist under the leadership of Superintendent Joseph Hawkins at Peter's Rock Family Worship Center. Tammie is a project manager and instructional coach for RCU at Mississippi State University. She is the executive producer of her own television show, The Tammie Tubbs Show which airs on Christian Television Network (WEPH TV 49). When not spending quality time and creating memories with her beautiful daughter Trinity, she's reaching the masses as a Television Personality, Evangelist, Educator, Certified Life Coach, Published Author, SMA Advocate and Entrepreneur. Tammie believes in healing and deliverance and the power of the Holy Spirit. Renew your Mind-Change Your Life!

www.tammietubbs.com

The Heart of a Leader Leadership Lessons

_____

_____

_____

_____

_____

_____

_____

_____

_____

_____

_____

_____

_____

_____

_____

_____

_____

_____

_____

_____

_____

_____

Tammie T. Tubbs

DIVINE LEADERSHIP: THE ART OF SELFLESS SERVICE

Wherever you are placed in your perspective roles, lead with integrity and treat others with dignity and respect. Do not waiver on your core principles and never feel pressured to step beneath who you were called to be, to get ahead. Your time will come, the promotion will be made available, and your gifts will make room for you! When you lead with a true servant's heart, there is no task too difficult to tackle. As always, put God first and lead with the foundation of faith and prayer. Remember that if you are placed in a position, it comes with much responsibility and sacrifice. I've always heard that Leaders are born, but I will venture to say effective Leaders are not born but created through determination, hard work, and service.

G. Allen

Whether working in a corporation or church administration, I have found that the true essence of a good leader is determined by what is on the inside of them: their heart posture, character, belief system, and core values. With Jesus being the ultimate and most effective leader of our time, it is very difficult to separate faith-based principles from corporate ideology; however, many times it is required in secular arenas.

President Dwight D. Eisenhower said, "Leadership is the art of getting someone else to do something you want done because he wants to do it." Through years of experience in student, church, civic, and workplace leadership, I have found this statement to ring true. My former manager mastered this idea by executing leadership in a way that the people he served would go above and beyond the call of duty to carry out the vision he set forth for the department. I, for one, felt loyal and inclined to work hard for this manager, willingly bending over backwards to support the needs of the department. For example, I would work during holidays and on weekends, stayed late, came to work on days off, and even interrupted vacation breaks to support the team. Truly, I did whatever it took for the department and manager to win and be successful. Now, I know the average person would refute this behavior or say 'forget that,' 'that sounds crazy,' or 'no job deserves that kind of effort,' but rest assured had it not been for the manager's excellent leadership ability and positive impact on me, I would have thought the same thing and my actions would have matched my sentiments. When I reflect on how my former manager leadership influenced me to respond in such a manner, the following thoughts and attributes come to mind:

1. **Communicate**. Communicate with staff daily about issues, needs, and/or concerns. Stay connected to the team by conducting weekly staff meetings and providing updates from management meetings. Additionally, weekly staff meetings also give team members an opportunity to share information and engage in healthy discussions and to stay

informed about any changes within the department. Although often overlooked, information sharing like forwarding emails with pertinent information or to give the team a heads up is a great way to keep the team in the know. I have experienced some leaders who treat employees like they are beneath them or subservient. This made the employees very tense and caused a lot of miscommunication between management and other staff members. It was always a "white elephant" in the room and when situations got testy, the lack of communication caused the biggest struggle. You get to choose what type of leader you want to be. Even if you are not as much of a communicator, seek to work on ways that the team feels heard and encourage an environment that allows open communication.

2. **Listen**. Listen to issues and concerns, then act on legitimate complaints when shown there is an issue. The best way to secure solid employees is to make them feel heard and seen, even when they are not talking. As stated earlier, communication is key to having a positive work environment and allows open dialogue between management and staff. Even if you are not in the corporate setting, listening to those who have been placed under your leadership is critical to have a solid team. It is easy for those in leadership to just "bark out" orders and tell people to do this and that, but what about the emotions and concerns of the workers? A listening ear can discourage mutiny in the work environment and even in volunteer situations. People feel better when they are heard, even if you as a leader cannot do something about the situation right at that moment. One of the worst feelings in the world is to try

your hardest and be "brushed off" when speaking directly to someone in leadership. This reaction will cause people to shy away from you when situations get sticky, prevent them from reaching their full potential, and most importantly cause them to not give their best efforts to the team. This all could be avoided if the leader understands that taking a few minutes out of day to "hear" someone will not cause the whole ship to sink.

3. **Care**. Express the human side by showing concern with the well-being of employees or key volunteers. It is important to understand and be sensitive to the needs of individuals on a team (ex. Time-off work, health issues, tend to family or kids). We all have to remember that we are human and nobody is a machine. With this being said, please keep that in mind as a leader. When you look at your staff,

don't expect them to function at 100% if they just had a death in the family or another major emergency that was unexpected. You as a leader want time off and have the luxury most times to take more rest or breaks than the team members. So if you know someone on the team is going through a difficult time, show that you care, ask how the company can support them, and allow them to take a break as company guidelines allow. These simple efforts can offer comfort to an employee who may be concerned about being present and providing for themselves and their family.

4. **Credibility.** Do what you say you are going to do and if you are unable let your team know. My former boss was a man of his word: he led by good example and practiced what he preached. I was able to confide in him about career ambitions or issues I had with other team members

without worrying about everything that I shared with him being repeated to others. We all know some managers who tell everything they hear and some who even add a little extra to make it sound good. This is not the way a good leader should conduct themselves. You do not have to be perfect, but strive to operate with integrity and remember that you were called to a higher standard; do not get caught up in futile conversations and office gossip. You should be a leader that appears neutral when it comes to employees and strive to be trustworthy and a person of high standards.

5. **Praise**. Acknowledging and celebrating accomplishments, saying thank you, saying Attagirl/Attaboy, publicly/openly acknowledging individual or team efforts. When you think about how many people in the faith-based community—as well as at work—have never been acknowledged

for their efforts, it is very disheartening. These individuals work tirelessly to help out and pitch in, but little to no appreciation can cause a team member to become disgruntled and discouraged. It would be wise and a good practice for a leader to celebrate those who work faithfully and are true team players. Regardless if you think everyone is doing a great job, celebrate those who are; for the ones who need to improve, try to look out for the times when they do operate in excellence and "make a big deal" out of that.

6. **Support**. It is critical for leaders to coach and mentor, while moving people in areas best suited to aid their skillset. Some people do not know their true abilities until someone encourages them and affirms they are capable. I remember starting at my current job and coming in without any experience in the field. To

ensure I felt comfortable and prepared for duties, management sent me to an array of training classes and provided resources so I could continue education. By having people in leadership supporting and encouraging me, I was reaffirmed that I could excel and tried very hard to not disappoint those who believed in me. It costs nothing to support someone who is assigned to your leadership, but it does produce greater new leaders!

7. **Humility.** Another trait that is sometimes seen with leaders is being overly concerned with perception over production. Have you ever seen someone in leadership that only wants recognition and does not want to do the work it takes to keep the show on the road? Yes, it brings more confusion than cohesiveness among the team. This can manifest itself negatively and is unhelpful. When a

leader becomes caught up in office gossip or makes it difficult on team members in an attempt to make himself feel greater, this does not mirror humility. This all can hinder the growth and development of the overall team. If you are concerned about how you look or will your name/picture be listed up front before everyone else, then you may need to examine your heart and motives. It is easy to feel as if you do not get recognized for your hard work, but truly your gifts and accomplishments will make room for you. At the right time you will be elevated for your work and your servant's heart. One of the most important lessons is to remain humble and work based on a foundation to help and uplift others. When you remain in balance by serving first and your legacy will go much farther. So do what it takes to get it done and your work will speak for itself!

8. **Serve First**. A good leader should encourage growth and support the goals of team members. The main focus should not be about making oneself look good, but identifying the best way to serve the team. This trait can be utilized with employees, volunteers, and other partners who are helping to accomplish a goal.

Fortunately, for many years I was guided by a leader with a very pronounced servant leadership style that inspired and motivated me daily to be better. What is a Servant Leader? A servant leader serves the people he/she leads. What does a Servant Leader do? Devote oneself to serving and meeting the needs of others, look at the needs of others, develop employees to bring out the best in them, coach others and encourage their self-expression, facilitate personal growth in all who work with them, and listen and build a sense of community.

In retrospect, I have adopted these attributes and used concepts in various leadership roles.

I diligently apply the concept of Servant Leadership in my everyday interaction with others is through relationship building. I engage with team members daily in various ways, brief small talk before addressing work-related issues. Additionally, I strive to meet the needs of colleagues and the company by being available to help team members inside and outside of my department—even when the tasks may not be in my "job description," I'm available to support others. One of the ultimate goals is to produce quality products on-time and on-cost which sometimes require us to do a few things outside of our tasking. With those you are leading, there is a difference between meeting needs vs. meeting wants.

Webster dictionary defines *need* as a lack of something wanted or deemed, i.e. *necessary to fulfill needs of the assignment.*

Webster dictionary defines want as to feel inclined; wish; a like, i.e. *we can stay at home if we want*. A want is something that one can exist without. It might affect one emotionally if a want is not met, but it is not crucial to one's survival.

Real Life Example: Water and food are needed. Lack of water and food will ultimately cause our demise. Soda is a want. We can live our entire lives without ever having a soda, but it won't kill us if we never drink soda.

Workplace Example: At first glance, some might see a promotion or pay raise as a need. And it might be in many cases. However, in some cases, it may be a want. The employee may need additional training, experience, people-focused skills, etc.

Consider this: when a manager thinks of promotion, she/he is focusing on the needs of the company. Is this the best person suited for this position as far as demeanor, qualifications, team-player, flexibility, leadership, etc. So, while the employee may see the promotion as a need and want, leaders must look at the larger vision.

Let's talk about relationship building for a moment. I'm sure hearing the phrase "relationship building" makes many of you feel uncomfortable because you are thinking too touchy, feely or that there must be an exchange of deep personal secrets; yet, this is not the case. I believe that relationship building is essential in any organization, especially the workplace. I have a general interest and concern about others. How is their day going? How was their weekend? What grade is Jane Doe in now? How's the home search coming along? How's this project? Can I assist you in any way? Following up, listening, and remembering things that are being shared is important, not because you are required to do so but because you care. *Be genuine*. The best leaders are concerned about their team and as stated earlier, they listen, but more importantly they hear their employees and take action. Leaders should know the challenges and day-to-day activities of all employees who report to them. Not only should leaders listen to employees, but taking time to visit work areas and interacting with them is significant. Leaders that take the time to see and understand daily tasks and challenges of team members accomplish two things: 1) It shows employees that their leaders want to learn what they do. 2) It creates an environment of mutual respect. Employees need to understand that what they do is important and relevant to the organization. Explore ways to help them see the bigger picture and explain how their daily work helps the organization achieve goals.

Some employees deal with character flaws and personal conflicts that can be detrimental to their success in working as a team. This includes characteristics like dishonesty, close-mindedness, selfishness, stubbornness, and refusal to be a part of a team. Variables such as the individuals' age, education, background, and socioeconomic status can all be factors in this. When dealing with people like this, being aware of their individuality and identifying ways to help them develop is the key.

How do you deal with communication issues? Communication issues must be addressed from the offset. The first step: allow people to talk. Have an option for group discussions, as well as individual discussions one-on-one. Once you start the conversation and get to the reasons that there were problems in the first place, it is a big step forward. What are some challenges you face in this area? Employees are used to the "status quo." They must feel confident that their opinions are not only listened to, but that the valid points will see results.

Wherever you are placed in your perspective roles, lead with integrity and treat others with dignity and respect. Do not waver on your core principles and never feel pressured to step beneath who you were called to be to get ahead. Your time will come, the promotion will be made available, your gifts will make room for you! When you lead with a true servant's heart there is no task too difficult to tackle. As always, put God first and lead with the foundation of faith and prayer. Remember that if you are placed in a position it comes with much responsibility and sacrifice. I've always heard that Leaders are born, but I will venture to say effective Leaders are not born but created through determination, hard work, and service. **The Heart of a Leader!**

Genice Allen

Leader in Corporate Leadership & Church Administration

Genice Allen is a nonprofit organizer, humanitarian, influencer, and administrative liaison. Having spent years in publishing, she is known best for creating success stories from sheer inspiration alone. Recognized for her contributions to the global aviation industry and communal leadership Genice spearheads projects centered on diversity & inclusion, educational advancement and economic opportunities for minorities and youth in rural communities.

Genice is a Mississippi native from a small town and a proud graduate of Mississippi State University with a Bachelor of Arts in Political Science. Currently, Genice works as a production engineering specialist for a leading aircraft manufacturer, where she creates work structures for the manufacturing, assembly, installation, design, and all technical aspects of helicopters. In addition, she has participated in trainings, development, and audits internationally.

Determined to build a legacy by implementing educational and economic opportunities, she developed a STEM Scholarship Fund for youth. When she is not busy advocating for causes, Genice Allen is a woman of great faith with a heart for family, friends, and community. She hopes to remain passionate about her call to servant leadership, and to connect with a body of influential leaders with a similar mandate.

LinkedIn: Genice Allen

Email: geniceallen@gmail.com

The Heart of a Leader Leadership Lessons

_____

_____

_____

_____

_____

_____

_____

_____

_____

_____

_____

_____

_____

_____

_____

_____

_____

_____

_____

_____

_____

DNA OF LEADERSHIP

I believe that one of the traits of a born leader is being well emotionally. The first characteristic of being whole is acknowledging what you are feeling. Those of us who are women in the African American community especially, do not want to be labeled as an angry black woman. However, I would like to give a biblical perspective from Ephesians 4:26 in the King James version. It states, "Be ye angry, and sin not: let not the sun go down upon your wrath." In other words, it means do not get a glock and put caps in his amen and hallelujah.

Beverly Banks

When you think of a leader, some may think of the outer appearances of an individual. The hair, makeup, designer clothes, shoes, the car he/she drives, and/or the multimillionaire homes they possessed. But sometimes we are just a shell that is empty and dead from the neck up.

I believe that one of the traits of a born leader is being well emotionally. What does it mean to be well emotionally? Because we are taught to be seen and not heard, one of the hosts of the Black CEO Morning Show, Dr. Stephanie Barnes, states on the show: "Take your voice off mute." Ladies and Gentlemen, this pandemic has shaken things to our core of how we interact with each other. The way we do business and how we use our busyness to hide the scars and pain causes people to suffer in silence. I believe God is using this time to help his children to be made whole in every area of life. These areas include being whole emotionally, financially, mentally, physically, sexually, and spiritual. Now, you are probably wondering who I am and what makes me an expert in telling you about being whole emotionally. My name is Beverly Banks, and I was one of those women who faked it until I made it instead of casting all my cares on him for he cares about me. I had been broken in every part of my life and I had learned to function in my dysfunction. I had to learn and unlearn some things that was etched in my soul. This chapter is to inspire and equip you in being a leader by taking care of yourself holistically. So let us take this journey together.

There are three characteristics a leader needs to become whole holistically and I would like to share them with you in this chapter.

I believe the first characteristic of being whole is acknowledging what you are feeling. Those of us who are women in the African American community especially do not want to be labeled as an angry black woman. However, I would like to give a biblical perspective from Ephesians 4:26 in the King James version. It states, "Be ye angry, and sin not: let not the sun go down upon your wrath." In other words, it means do not get a *glock* and put caps in his *amen* and *hallelujah*. We have every right to be mad when we are mistreated, verbally abused, seen and treated as sexual beings instead of the intelligent, strong, fearfully and wonderfully made women we are. We are taught sometimes that this behavior is acceptable, when in hindsight, we learn to function in what we believe is normal. Some women are functioning based on what this world has taught and how one was supposed to act, behave, or respond instead of what God has said and how He created us to be.

Some leaders are made, and some leaders are born with greatness. Some forget the greatness planted in them because we have not dealt with the brokenness, disappointments, and other generational curses that were and are being passed down from generations to generations. When we face our cycles, patterns, and coping mechanisms that we use to endure life, we can start enjoying our life. This brings me to my second point in being emotionally well.

Take responsibility for your emotionally healing. I know for a long time I blamed everyone and everything for being in pain expect for me. Please do not take this the wrong way, but I ask you to take an honest assessment of your life and see what part you play in it. For a long time, I struggled to express my wants and needs in a constructive and honest manner because the adults in my life were not very nurturing. I had to submit under authority even when the individuals were not well themselves. We have been taught what goes on in our house stays in our house, even if it is killing us. I did not have the support and the guidance to become an emotionally balanced person, but it did not mean I had to stay in a valley.

The third and final point in becoming an emotionally well-balanced person is to seek professional help and set healthy boundaries for yourself. What really makes me mad in the African American community is how we belittle and shame one other when we share that we are seeking counseling from a mental health professional. To me, it represents strength when you admit you need help and you want to be made whole. If a person demeans you this way, seek new friends who will love your faults and all. One thing I love to do is journal. When you write things in a journal, you do not have to be biblical, grammatical, or politically correct. You can release all of the stress and tensions that you may have stored up because many of us do not have a safe environment to relieve all of the emotional baggage we have carried for so long. One of my tips when seeking a professional licensed therapist is to ask questions. This is another one of my pet peeves. One of my favorite scriptures is Hosea 4:6 when it says, "My people perish for the lack of knowledge." We need God's knowledge to be the leader that He calls us to be. I know I stated three characteristics, but I wanted to add a bonus.

Seek God's wisdom because you need wisdom and guidance when making decisions for yourself and others. You will need to know the challenges, the pros, and the cons of a project or task set in front you. You have to be objective and learn how not to take things so personally. We will eventually deal with other personalities and individuals who are not like us, but you are up for the challenge.

Beverly Banks
Leader in Emotional Wellness

Beverly Banks is employed with the government in the District of Columbia; her passion is to help women get free emotionally. She specializes in emotional healing.

Ms. Beverly Banks has a story to tell and when she fully releases what is in her mouth; watch out to those who wanted to muzzle and keep her silent. You can hear the comedic relief in her writing and feel her passion and zeal for emotional healing in leaders.

Beverly Banks

https://www.facebook.com/beverly.banks.75

https://www.instagram.com/babanks1/

The Heart of a Leader Leadership Lessons

_____

_____

_____

_____

_____

_____

_____

_____

_____

_____

_____

_____

_____

_____

_____

_____

_____

_____

_____

_____

HEART LESSONS TO LEARN

Do not bypass professionalism in ministry. Many people want to bypass expectations, protocol, and professionalism to let God use them. God is a God of order, so if it's a mess, it's probably not God using them. Some people want the full benefits of a blessing but follow through on half of the requirements. Be on time, meet deadlines, communicate, respond when asked questions, submit to leadership, dress accordingly, speak to others the way you want to be addressed in a crowd, carry your own weight, and follow through on your commitment. And if anything changes and you are no longer able to carry out your obligation or duty, tell those in charge in a timely manner.

Simene' Walden

As an educator and teacher by vocation for 16 years, I understand firsthand your leadership starts on day one when you have students in front of you. They are looking for you to lead them and teach them. And guess what, younger students are no different from adult students.

Even if you are not given the title of leader, you are absolutely leading them. The question is where are we leading them and how are we leading them? Men and women who are taught or following a leader look to you for guidance. It is our responsibility to lead them well.

When I started serving in ministry, I realized the same work ethic and standards that I had in education and teaching were the same standards plus that I needed to keep while serving the people of God.

The heart of a leader is more about intent and will than about skill and education. Good leadership starts with a commitment in your heart. John Maxwell quotes out of his book, *The 21 Indispensable Qualities of a Leader:* "The real measure of commitment is action."

You have heard from top leaders in their industry already in this anthology. If you just skipped to my chapter, go back and re-read everyone's chapter. It adds value to the overall premise of this message. Besides, I want you to be committed to action so you can take action.

What I found that worked in education also worked in ministry. What I did only in ministry, I found worked also in education. Obviously, you must be wise as a serpent and harmless as a dove, but great leadership is great leadership.

Below are twenty heart lessons to learn as a new and emerging leader. Take what you need, recycle the rest, and pass on what you have learned.

I look forward to hearing how your leadership as an individual, group, organization, school, or ministry has been impacted and you have seen tangible results because of the action taken and the work that was done.

Please share your testimonials either by email or tag any of us on social media so we too can be encouraged that what we took time to pen is helping people that we may never get to meet.

20 Heart Lessons to Learn as A New & Emerging Leader

1. Do not think your way is the only or best way.

2. Get help. Do not do it alone if you do not have to. Work with those serving and leading with you but make sure you are carrying your weight.

3. Go with only those God has chosen to go with you.

4. Be honest and truthful about where you are and what you can do.

5. Be submitted to authority and the leadership over you.

6. Be courteous, fair, and respectful to those who serve with you.

7. Those who are under your leadership are equally valuable as you are. You are just the voice some people will hear but the answers and outcomes collectively should

come from the team if you have one and if it calls for that. Sometimes as a leader, you will have to make an executive decision and stick with it.

8. There will be times when you will have to make an executive decision and stand behind it, regardless of what others are saying if God gave you the answer. Everyone may not like it or agree, but if you believe that is what is best, stick to it.

9. Be ok with being in isolation at times. You should not be isolated all the time, but there will be times when you will be alone. It may come from a personal choice and other times it may come from people distancing themselves not understanding some of the decision you have made. Other times, people become envious of you doing what they do not have the courage to do.

10. You are not perfect, and you will make mistakes, but God is a God who can redeem your time and forgive you. Sometimes people are not so forgiving or as quick to forgive you, but be honest about your mistakes. Do you know your flaws look flawless to other people? So don't shy away from them: learn from them and keep growing.

11. Practice self-control or you will self-destruct. When you do not give a response, that is still a response. Everything does not need a response. Focus on the main things that what will be important in another year or so. No is indeed a complete sentence and thought. There is no explanation needed but great leaders will sometimes make allowances to explain as a courtesy and teaching moment. They do not do it of fear or guilt. There will be times when you need to be transparent about decisions made.

12. Make sure you are accountable to someone. The greatest leaders have the greatest accountability. There has to be someone who can correct and encourage you on your lifestyle, behavior, and decision making at all times.

13. Holy Spirit is the Spirit of Truth and you need to go to Him for truth at all times. He told me once: "There are always three sides to a story. Your side, their side, and my side. I am the Spirit of Truth. I know the intents, motives, and reasons why people do what they do, say what they say, or act like they act. Come to me. I am The Spirit of Truth."

14. All people have sinned and come short of the glory of God. Allow room for error but do not let sin or error go without being addressed. Unresolved issues spread and destroy.

15. Be inviting so people will feel free to come to you about any issues or concerns.

16. Create a culture that is inviting in case individuals would rather go to someone else about their concerns. This is not a gossip or grip session so make sure those you appoint or who have self-appointed themselves share the same spirit and ideology as you.

17. Be professional when needed and necessary. Remember before you are a leader, you are a person and people connect with people they can relate to. Be human and don't be so hard on yourself, but also know who can see how much of your non-professional side. Some people will use it against you later.

18. Do not bypass professionalism in ministry. Many people want to bypass expectations, protocol, and

professionalism to let God use them. God is a God of order, so if it's a mess, it's probably not going using them. Some people want the full benefits of a blessing but follow through on half of the requirements. Be on time, meet deadlines, communicate, respond when asked questions, submit to leadership, dress accordingly, speak to others the way you want to be addressed in a crowd, follow through on your commitment, if anything changes and you are no longer able to carry out your obligation or duty, tell those in charge in a timely manner, and carry your own weight. You are as strong as the weakest person on your team. Time to build everyone's capacity.

19. Do not become ensnared by a title which is a fancy word for a label. Do not become proud because you are leading. The same way God calls us up, He can call us down. May we always be promoted and

not demoted. God resists the proud but gives grace to the humble. Labels only matter when you display the characteristics of that label. If you do not fit that label or title of leader, you are an imposter, fake, and phony. Just because you hit moments of obscurity and uncertainty does not mean you are not a leader. It means you are growing your capacity and expanding for more.

20.   Humble Yourself. In due time, you will be exalted to another level. Serve well where you are.

Simene' Walden

Leader in Marketplace Ministry

Simene' Walden, also known as The Student Teacher, is a Culture and Morale Specialist, Educator, Speaker, Trainer, Book Publisher, and an Amazon Best Selling Author. She helps educators and leaders tell their stories unapologetically through written and verbal communication. Simene' is the visionary behind The Heart of a Leader Anthology along with two other anthologies: *Unmasked to Heal* and *Unmute Yourself*.

The ABC's of Simene' The Student Teacher are A for Academics, B for Books & The Bible, & C for Coaching & Crucial Conversations. Simene' Walden taught Middle School English Language Arts for 16 years. She is certified as a Youth Mental Health First Aid from The National Council for Mental Well Being and a Practitioner of Social Emotional Learning. She is also ACES (Adverse Childhood Experiences) and Trauma Informed Care Trained. She now serves schools and organizations in the capacity of professional developments, speaking engagements, trainings for their staff, and school assemblies for students.

Simene' assists others in speaking their stories by hosting live and in person events, conducting online radio interviews, featuring other speakers during her social media events, providing opportunities for authors to write their own books to becoming co-authors in her author lead anthologies, or other being featured on her written blog.

Simene' has been featured in The Roanoke Chowan News Herald, Good Morning Washington, FOX 40 News, ABC 21WFMJ, FOX 43 WTNZ, Topeka Magazine, Voyage ATL, and the Glambitious Magazine just to name a few. The Student Teacher understands the power of your thought life and heart posture that impacts your speech. Simene' Walden speaks life and has already helped over 300+ women and a few distinguished men to do just that. If you are looking for just a publisher, Simene' is not the one, but if you are looking for a publisher who will not just help you publish your story, but will help you carry your story, connect with her today.

Simene' assists new writers and authors with faith-based book coaching and publishing, text editing, braille transcription, speech & storytelling assistance, testimonial cultivation, and course & curriculum development.

Simene' also provides small group coaching for those who are ready to unmute and unmask. She hosts masterclasses and courses for those who want to write and publish. Unmuting and Unmasking your story or part of what leads you to Becoming Pretty Healed & Handsomely Whole.

Pretty Healed & Handsomely Whole apparel line was birthed in prayer. It was through reading the Word where Simene' would find phrases and slogans that stood out to her. Those words became daily affirmations and declarations.

http://www.prettyhealed.com

simene@simenewalden.com

https://www.facebook.com/simene/

https://www.facebook.com/thestudenteacher

http://www.twitter.com/@simenewalden

https://www.linkedin.com/in/simenewalden/

http://instagram.com/simenewalden

The Heart of a Leader Leadership Lessons

_____

_____

_____

_____

_____

_____

_____

_____

_____

_____

_____

_____

_____

_____

_____

_____

_____

_____

_____

_____

www.ingramcontent.com/pod-product-compliance
Lightning Source LLC
Chambersburg PA
CBHW060228030426
42335CB00014B/1369